LOOK AT
COLOR AND
CAMOUFLAGE

Franklin Watts Inc.
387 Park Avenue South
New York
N.Y. 10016

© 1989 Franklin Watts Limited

Editor: Ruth Thomson

Design: K and Co.
Consultant: Julian Hector
Illustrations: Simon Roulstone
Typeset by Lineage, Watford
Printed in Italy
by G. Canale & C.S.p.A., Turin

Picture credits:
Heather Angel 18, 19, 26b, 26c, 27a, 27b, 27c, 28a, 28b, 29c
Bruce Coleman 10, 14, 22, 23
Chris Fairclough 9
Oxford Scientific Films 16b, 17, 24, 25
Neil Thomson 5c
Science Photo Library 5a
Survival Anglia 20, 28c, 29b
Peter Newark's Military Pictures 4b
Zefa 4a, 5b, 6a, 6b, 7a, 7b, 8, 11, 12, 13, 15, 16a, 21, 26a, 29a

Library of Congress Cataloguing-in-Publication Data
Thomson, Ruth.
    Color and camouflage / Ruth Thomson.
      p.   cm.—(Look at)
    Includes index.
    Summary: An introduction, in simple text and photographs, to the
physical characteristics and behavior of a variety of animals.
    ISBN 0-531-14000-8
    1. Animal behavior—Juvenile literature.   2. Camouflage (Biology)—
Juvenile literature. [1. Animals—Habits and behaviour.
2. Camouflage (Biology)]   I. Title.
QL751.5.T46   1990
591.57'2—dc20   89-36215
                                            CIP
                                            AC

LOOK AT
COLOR AND
CAMOUFLAGE

Rachel Wright

FRANKLIN WATTS

London • New York • Sydney • Toronto

We wear colored clothes
for different reasons.

Soldiers wear colors that match
their surroundings.
This makes it harder
for their enemies to spot them.

In the past, soldiers wore bright
red uniforms to scare their enemies,
and to be seen.

We recognize doctors
by their white coats.

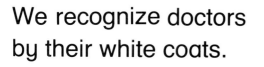

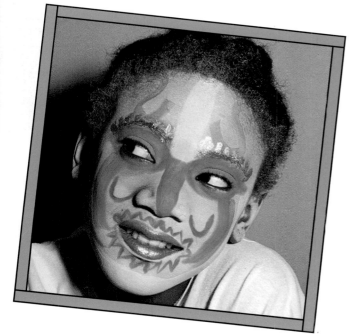

We dress up and color our faces
to get ourselves noticed.

Animals use their colors and patterns
in similar ways.
Do you know why some animals are patterned
and others are not?
Or why some are brightly colored
and others are not?

Field mouse

Butterfly fish

Kingfisher

Leopard

7

Many birds and insects see in color.
They can see a bigger range of colors than humans.
Their coloring helps them to recognize or signal to each other.

Parrots

Most mammals, like dogs and cats,
don't see in color.
They see only pale colors or shades of gray.
Color is not important to them.
This is why so many are dully colored.

Labrador

Some animals have bright colors
to attract a mate.
Male birds of paradise dance and show off
their colored feathers to the females.

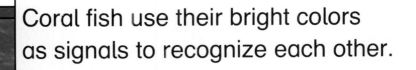

Coral fish use their bright colors as signals to recognize each other.

Poisonous insects and those with a sting
are often black and yellow.
These colors warn their enemies
not to attack them.

Bumble bee

Hover fly

Some harmless insects are
black and yellow too.
They are called mimics.
Their colors fool their enemies
into thinking they are dangerous.

The peacock butterfly also uses color
to protect itself.
With its wings folded, it looks helpless.

If it is disturbed,
it will suddenly open its wings
to reveal two big, colored eyespots.
These frighten away its enemy.

Tiger

Texas horned lizard

Many animals have colors that match
their surroundings.
These make it difficult for them to be seen.
This is called camouflage.

Insect-eating bats search for food at night.
Their dark coloring makes it hard for their prey to spot them against the night sky.

Nightjar

Hunted animals also use camouflage.
Female birds are often drab,
so that they will be camouflaged
when sitting on their nests.

Flatfish live mainly on the seabed.
Their markings look like specks of sand,
so their outline is hard to see.

Zebras graze and move about in herds.
From a distance their stripes appear to blend.
This protects the herd from attack.

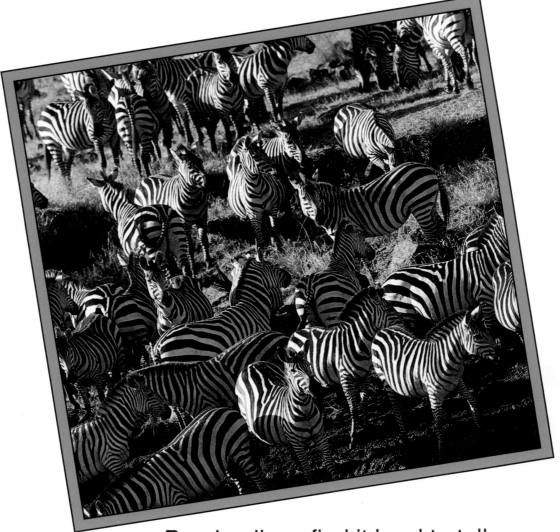

Preying lions find it hard to tell
one zebra from another.

Arctic animals have light-colored coats.
This is useful camouflage in the snow,
for both hunters and the hunted.
This Arctic fox is a hunter.

Some creatures change their color
as they grow older.
Baby tapirs are patterned, which helps
to camouflage them in the undergrowth.
Adult tapirs have dark coats,
so they won't be seen when they feed at night.

Some male freshwater fish become brightly colored when they are very angry or excited.
Their color fades as they calm down.

Some animals that live in the Arctic all the time,
change color in summer and winter.
This way they are camouflaged
all year round.

The white-tailed ptarmigan is white
in winter...

and changes to brown as summer approaches.

Chameleons can change their color
to match their surroundings...

so can bell-frogs.

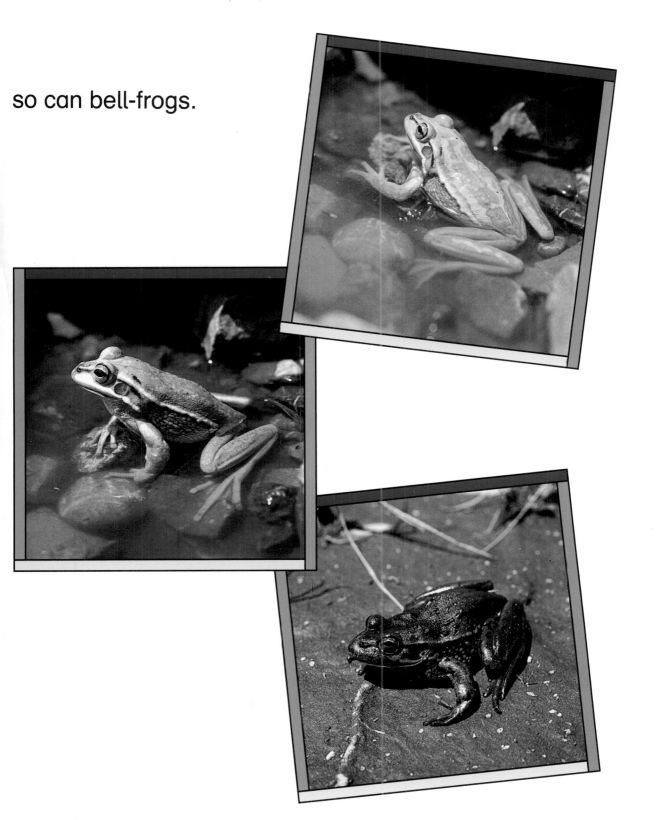

In each picture, there is
a well-camouflaged animal.
Can you see
where they are hiding?

Viper

Lynx

Leaf fish

Oak beauty moth

Ptarmigan

Crayfish

Do you know?

● The color of birds' eggs often helps to camouflage them.

Nightjars, terns and plovers lay their eggs out in the open, not in a nest. The color of the eggs matches the ground on which they are laid.

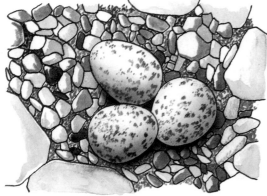

The wood pigeon's eggs are white. Their flimsy nests have see-through bottoms. If you stood underneath the nest and looked up, the eggs are difficult to see.

Owls' eggs are glossy white, so that their parents can see them in the dark.

● Some animals change color as the moisture in the air changes. Toads become paler in dry, warm weather. Pale colors reflect more heat and this helps to keep them cool.

● Decorator crabs have tiny, curved bristles on their shells. Bits of seaweed and other materials hook on to their bristles. This helps to camouflage them.

● As far as anyone knows, octopuses cannot see in color. This is strange, since they are able to turn from white to red in seconds.

● Many fish are brightly colored. In general, the more brightly colored a fish, the more aggressive it is.

Things to do

● Keep a camouflage scrapbook. Collect pictures of animals camouflaged against different backgrounds. Make separate sections for those that change color with the seasons, those that change color with age and those that change color with mood.

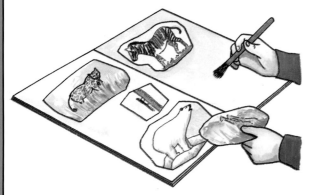

● Draw or model some scenery. Add an animal or bird whose colors blend in with those you have already used.

● When you next visit the zoo, make a note of all the brightly colored animals and birds that you see. Try to find out why they are so brightly colored.

Words and sayings

Can you find out what these words and sayings mean?

color blind
false colors
off color
colorful
colorless
colorfast
color up
high color
primary colors

To lose color
To come out in one's true colors
To come off with flying colors
To nail one's colors to the mast
To eat one's colors
Fear no colors
Under color of

Index

Arctic birds 24, 25
Arctic fox 21

Bats 17
Bee 12
Birds 7, 8, 10, 18, 24, 25, 29, 30
Butterfly 14, 15

Cats 9
Camouflage 16, 17, 18, 19, 20, 21, 22,
    24, 25, 27, 28, 29, 30
Chameleons 26
Color change 22, 23, 24, 25, 26, 27, 31
Color vision 8, 9
Crayfish 29

Doctor 5
Dog 9

Eggs 30

Field mouse 6
Fish 6, 11, 19, 23, 28, 29
Fly 13
Frogs 27

Hoverfly 13

Insects 8, 12, 13

Kingfisher 7

Labrador 9
Leopard 7
Lizard 16
Lynx 28

Mimics 13
Moth 29

Nightjar 18, 30

Parrots 8
Ptarmigan 24, 25, 29

Soldiers 4

Tapir 22
Tiger 16
Toad 30

Viper 28

Zebra 20